Little Pebble™

MIGHTY MILITARY MACHINES

Destroyers

A 4D BOOK

by Matt Scheff

PEBBLE
a capstone imprint

Download the Capstone **4D** app!

- Ask an adult to download the Capstone 4D app.

- Scan the cover and stars inside the book for additional content.

When you scan a spread, you'll find fun extra stuff to go with this book! You can also find these things on the web at www.capstone4D.com using the password: destroyers.01105

Little Pebble is published by Pebble
1710 Roe Crest Drive, North Mankato,
Minnesota 56003
www.mycapstone.com

Library of Congress Cataloging-in-Publication Data
Library of Congress Cataloging-in-Publication data is available from the Library of Congress website.

ISBN 978-1-9771-0110-5 (hardcover)
ISBN 978-1-9771-0116-7 (paperback)
ISBN 978-1-9771-0122-8 (eBook PDF)

Editorial Credits
Marissa Kirkman, editor; Heidi Thompson, designer;
Jo Miller, media researcher; Tori Abraham, production specialist

Photo Credits
U.S. Navy photo by MC2 Huey D. Younger Jr., 11, MC2 Jon Dasbach, cover, MC3 Bill Dodge, 21; Wikimedia: Hpeterswald, 15, U.S. Navy photo, 5, MC2 Edward Guttierrez III, 19, MC2 James R. Evans, 7, MC2 Jay C. Pugh, 17, MC3 Bill Dodge, 13, PH2 John L. Beeman, 9
Design Elements: Shutterstock: Zerbor

Printed and bound in China.
000309

Table of Contents

Strong Ships

Look! What is it?

It is a navy ship.

It is a destroyer.

At Sea

These ships are big.

They are strong.

They lead the fleet.

The fleet sails out to sea.

The crew runs the ship.

Destroyers keep ships safe.

They look for enemy ships.

Parts

Boom! Blast! Bang!

These ships have big guns.

The hull is the ship's body.

It is made of steel.

hull

The engines burn fuel.

Zoom!

The ship goes fast.

Look up!

The mast is tall.

mast

The crew works hard.

They keep the navy safe.

Glossary

crew—a team of people who work together

engine—a machine that makes the power needed to move something

fleet—a large group of ships that travel together

hull—the main body of a boat or ship

mast—the part of a destroyer that rises high above the hull; the mast contains most of the ship's instruments

navy—the branch of the military that fights on water

steel—a strong type of metal

Read More

Marx, Mandy R. *Amazing U.S. Navy Facts*. Amazing Military Facts. North Mankato, Minn.: Capstone Press, 2017.

Murray, Julie. *United States Navy*. U.S. Armed Forces. Minneapolis: Abdo Kids, 2015.

Reed, Jennifer. *The U.S. Navy*. The U.S. Military Branches. North Mankato, Minn.: Capstone Press, 2018.

Internet Sites

Use FactHound to find Internet sites related to this book.

Visit *www.facthound.com*
Just type in 9781977101105 and go.

Super-cool stuff! Check out projects, games and lots more at
www.capstonekids.com

Critical Thinking Questions

1. What is the tallest part of a destroyer?

2. What is the hull made of?

3. Who runs a destroyer?

Index